# Teddy's Tail

The Wit and Wisdom of an F.O.T.
(Fat Orange Tabby)

**Written by Bette-Jean Coderre**

Illustrated by Karen S. Marshall

Teddy's Tail
The Wit and Wisdom of an F.O.T.
(Fat Orange Tabby)

Copyright © 2014 by Bette-Jean Coderre
All Rights Reserved
ISBN-13 : 978-0615976488
ISBN-10 : 0615976484
CreateSpace, North Charleston, SC

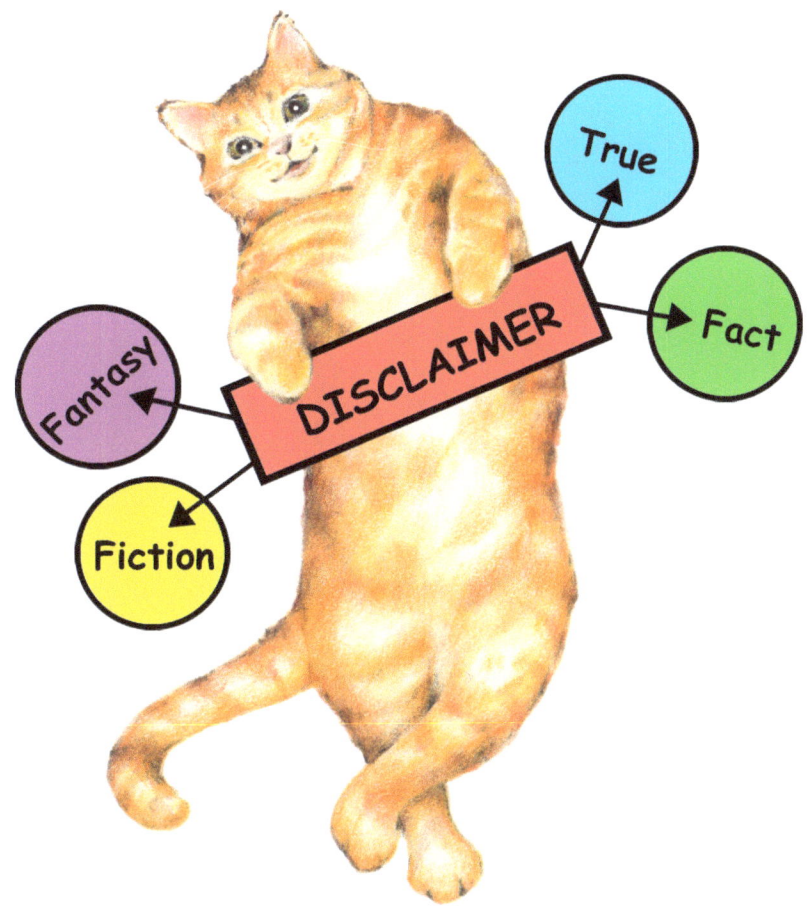

This book is a work of non-fiction depending on whose point of view is being offered.

From my point of view, it is a true tale.

From others' point of view, it is purely a fictitious tale fabricated by one fat, fabulous feline.

**FABULOUS !**     At least we agree on something.     **PURRRRRRRRrrrrr……**

 IN LOVING MEMORY

In loving memory
of my Grand-MeeMee,
Olive Coderre Picozzi
who loved me unconditionally,
even though she called me a
"Little Dickens"
and
"That Little Imp."

Theodore Coderre

## DEDICATION

"Teddy's Tail" would never have come to life without the help of a very special person.

This person epitomizes the promises of her veterinarian oath:

*"...I will practice my profession consciously with dignity.*

*The health of my patients,*

*the best interest of their owners...will be my primary consideration...*

*I will uphold and strive to advance the honor and noble traditions of the veterinary profession..."*

It is with a grateful heart, that I dedicate this book

to Teddy's veterinarian,

**DR. JO MICHAELSON, D.V.M.**

| | | | |
|---|---|---|---|
| Prologue: | Feline-icity | pg. | 1 |
| Chapter 1 | Catnapped! | pg. | 9 |
| Chapter 2 | Scheme | pg. | 23 |
| Chapter 3 | Sticks and Stones | pg. | 26 |
| Chapter 4 | PETulant | pg. | 28 |
| Chapter 5 | Alias | pg. | 30 |
| Chapter 6 | Forewarning! | pg. | 34 |
| Chapter 7 | Exultant! | pg. | 35 |
| Chapter 8 | Aerobics | pg. | 36 |
| Chapter 9 | Paws in Praise | pg. | 38 |
| Chapter 10 | Verdict | pg. | 41 |
| Chapter 11 | Santa-Clawsing | pg. | 43 |
| Chapter 12 | Anxiety | pg. | 45 |
| Chapter 13 | Treasured Friends | pg. | 46 |
| Chapter 14 | Teddy-Tail Flashbacks | pg. | 48 |
| Epilogue: | Utopia | pg. | 58 |

PROLOGUE

   FELINE-ICITY

## ME-YOW!

Once there was a little orange kitty.

His name was Teddy.

He loved to purr.

PURR PURR PURR PURR PURR PURR

Purr Purr Purr

PURRR

PURR PURRR

purr PURR

purrrrrrr

purrrrrrrrrrrr ....

Purr Purr Purr

purrrrrrrrrrrr ....

He loved to play.

He loved to eat.

He loved ADVENTURE !!!

To him life was one big celebration,

AND TEDDY was not going to miss a moment of it.

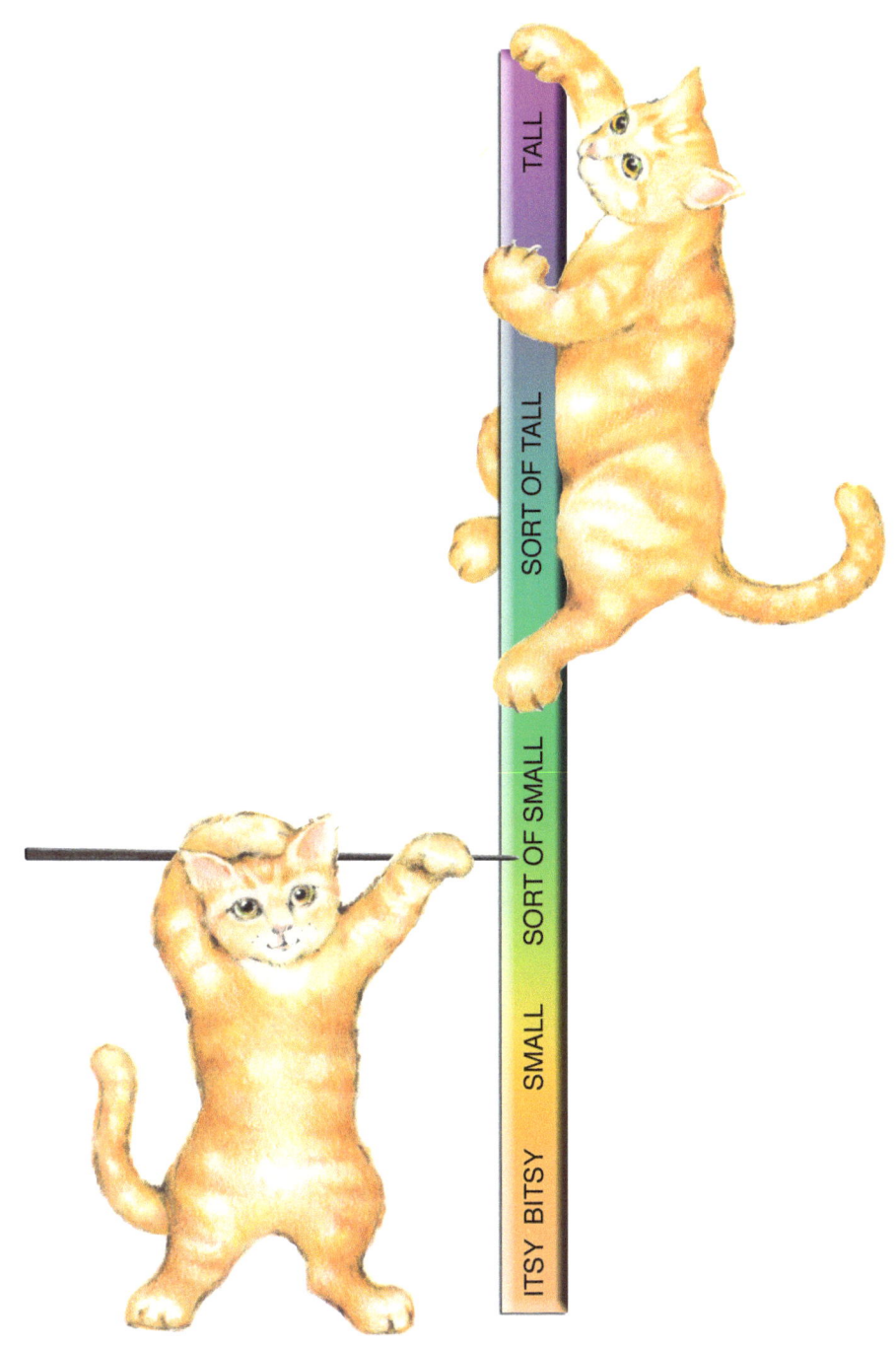

Teddy grew,

and grew,

and grew.

The spirited kitty became an ingenious cat.

He watched educational programs.

**He learned to use his MeeMee's computer.**

**He took classes online.**

He graduated and put his paws to creative writing.

"What should be my theme?" Teddy asked himself. Teddy thought, and thought, and thought.

"Aha!" he concluded. "I will write letters to Doctor Jo Michaelson

BECAUSE

the pen is mightier than the paw."

# CHAPTER 1
## CATNAPPED !

HELP !   HELP !!   HELLLPP !!!

I have been CATNAPPED !

I have been put into a little locked cell.

There is no food,

no water,

no litterbox,

only bars and cramped space.

If my human knew this, she would be furious. She would be crying. She would do all in her power to get me back.

WAIT A MINUTE ........

    HMMM !

I do believe it was my human, my beloved MeeMee, who did this terrible thing. Why would she do this to me, her Darling Boy?

OH, NO - O - O - O ! I bet she is taking me to the Montville Animal Hospital. I must have an appointment with the veterinarian, Dr. Jo Michaelson.

**Please, SOMEONE, ANYONE, help me to escape! I will make it worth your while. I will give you lots and lots of canned cat food. Cat food comes in several brands and varieties. You can have all one kind or a mixed selection of the delectable, delicious flavors. Savor the moment. Choose your preferences. It matters NOT how much I have to give you. JUST SET ME FREEEeeeee !!!**

**Too late! I'm in the car!    Destination: TORTUREVILLE !!!!    Oh, I mean the vet's.**

"Hello, Teddy. Come right in," the doctor coos upon my arrival. Fiddlesticks ! She doesn't fool me one bit. I know pretty soon she will be pricking, prodding, AND weighing me. Inside we go to let the receptionist check our information. She usually double checks to make sure everything is accurate. Once when MeeMee was asking the receptionist a question, I reversed some digits of the phone number. Right away she noticed it. Fortunately, I have a reprieve. MeeMee usually goes very early for my appointment. In reality, this is not such a bad thing.

Arriving before my scheduled time is an entertaining experience.

Here, I enjoy and encounter other extraordinary and remarkable animals.

Montville Animal Hospital is a virtual animal amusement park.

Much to my delight and mischievous personality, Dr. Michaelson's waiting room is full of several pleasurable things to do. There are things to color, other cats to chatter with ... AND ... doggies to frolic with ... and/or observe the in-depth scientific carefully researched thesis studying the complex illusive problematic causes in canine behavior. Hmmm ...

                                                        Of course, if you prefer ...

there are books to read,

fish to observe and catch,

and escape routes to plan !

**FANTASTIC !!!**

Currently in the waiting room are two dogs, two other cats, and a canary. I cast a glance at the other animals. The other cats are cautious but have opted to take a catnap. The canary is chirping merrily. The dogs are friendly and affable. Just for the fun of it, I pretend I'm a maestro conducting their wagging tails. The dogs, Roxy and Tucker, happily play the game with me. Their soprano and alto voices join together and fill the room with harmonious song.

What a delightful time I am having!  THEN the door to Tortureville Room #2 opens.

Out comes the vet tech, Reneé.  All of us stand at attention.  "Teddy !" she calls.

The other animals sigh in relief.  In her hand she is holding my RECORD.

On the vet's record I am listed as a DSH, a Domestic Short Hair. A lot of people just call me a tabby cat. I think a cat by any other name is still a cat, a member of the Royal Family of Felines.

So the first thing the vet tech does is check my weight. I try to hypnotize her by projecting the thought, "Keep this between us. Keep this between us."     FAT CHANCE !
She totally ignores me. I watch her closely. Jeepers! She's an informant. Not only does she tell MeeMee but she also writes it down. It is now on my permanent record. I would growl at her but I realize she is just doing her job.

By the time Dr. Michaelson comes in, my dander is up. I mean that in more ways than one. I am exhausted from trying to mesmerize the vet tech by pleading, "Please put me back in my carrier. Take me home!     Taaaaaaaaaaake meeeeeeee hoooooooooome !!!!!!"

She pretends not to understand me as she is in collusion with the vet. "Great minds run in the same channel." This is perplexing. I have a great mind. Most assuredly, I am not running in their channel. I am an anxious patient pleading for liberation.

Going to the vet is a frequent occurrence. MeeMee takes me to the vet every time I sneeze or blink an eye. To tell you the truth, Dr. Michaelson is not only very knowledgeable but she is also very cordial. She glances at me, smiles sweetly, tries to soothe my troubled soul, and asks, "How are you doing, Teddy?"
I look up at her and think, "Dr. Michaelson, I am here so often I consider you a FRIEND. May I call you Jo?

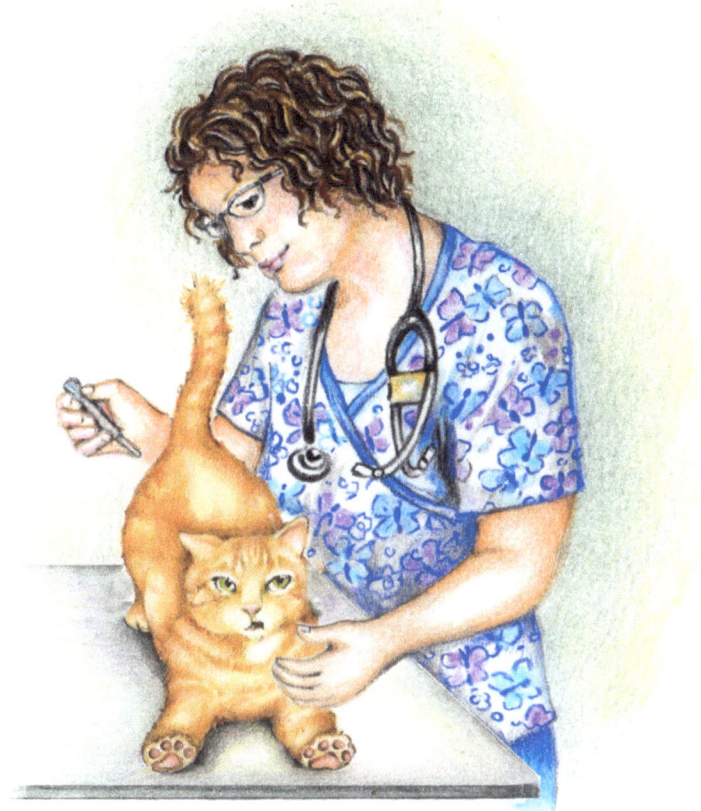

Hey,  FRRRIEND !!!
Watch where you're putting that thermometer !"

After Dr. Michaelson checks me out, the vet tech picks up my carrier. I make a bounding leap for it. They all laugh and fall backwards slightly. Do they assume that I am not cognizant of my actions? Unsurprisingly, I did not jump joyfully OUT of the carrier, just BACK into it.

The vet tech is cheerfully chuckling and bursts into a spontaneous song:
"He flies through the air with the greatest of ease,
That daring fast Teddy is creating a breeze."

Granted, it must have been comical to see a cat soaring through the air, but why would they suppose any cat would choose to remain on the examination table? Would you?

I ask you, "Do humans jump up and down with joy when the doctor says they have to have a colonoscopy?" Is this their response?

"Oh Doctor, I am so delighted. I am going right out to celebrate by having a delicious milkshake."

HOGWASH !

They drink all right but it is no milkshake.

Why can't they understand that we cats do not enjoy being examined? We would rather relax in the security and safety of our own homes.

## CHAPTER 2
### SCHEME

As you may have already surmised, I have launched a scheme which will make Dr. Michaelson reject the notion of ever imprisoning me again.

Here is my strategy:
- Get on the GOOD SIDE of Dr. Michaelson.
- Write her letters.
- Appeal to her wry sense of humor.
- Make her more aware of my intelligence.
- Remain vigilant.

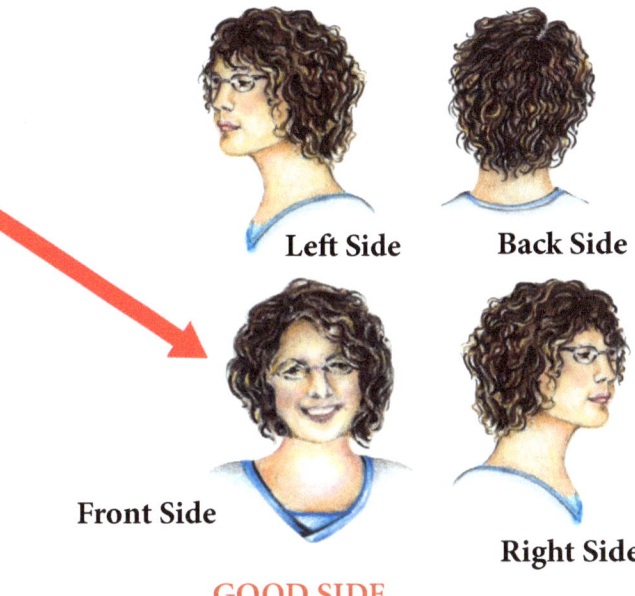

Left Side   Back Side

Front Side

Right Side

GOOD SIDE

She will not refuse to see me when MeeMee calls her office. Rats to that woman!

She is too well mannered to say to MeeMee, "No, you cannot bring Teddy in today. It is not unusual for a cat to sneeze occasionally."

Her thoughtfulness is beginning to grate on my nerves. Unfortunately, it is also making me reassess my plan and just let her perform her job.

NO !         NO !!         **NO !!!**

Persist, I must !     Compose the letters.     Keep her amused.

Dr. Michaelson will then acknowledge me as the funny feline that I am, despite my constant hissing and growling when I am there. I do have my pride.

To execute this plan will be effortless. For years I have had practice with the computer. Every time my MeeMee turned on her computer, up I would jump onto the keyboard. Little did she realize there was a "method to my madness". She thought I was just being charming, wanting to be near her at all times. In reality, I was learning the keyboard and other computer skills.

## Olé !!

TEDDY the MISCHIEVOUS has become THEODORE the WISE.

Obstacles ?   NONE !

        Running the PRINTER ?

                Piece of CAKE !

Faith "taught" me that when I was just an itsy bitsy kitsy.   Mew !   Mew !!   Mew !!!

The computer IS mightier than the paw.

I, Theodore, will inform Dr. Michaelson that our relationship has changed.  It will now be a written one and not a personal one.  NO EXAMS OR SHOTS FOR ME !!  If she insists on my continuing to have physical examinations, I'M READY !

I have been rehearsing my hissing and growling and can hiss-growl in tenor and baritone.  After all, I cannot take this lying down.

I have unremittingly been practicing my signatures:

*Theodore*

*Theodore*

*Theodore*

Will she know who that is?

On second thought, I feel the letters should be signed **Teddy**.  Yes ! Teddy, it is.  Doesn't that sound cute and innocent?

Purrrr !  Purrrrr !!  Purrrrrrr !!!

After all, "You can catch more flies with honey than you can with vinegar."  And I can be a real
## HONEY.

# CHAPTER 3
## STICKS & STONES

Dear Dr. Michaelson,

This morning, ONCE AGAIN, I was in your office. I heard you. Do you not know that I am sensitive? You were telling MeeMee that I need to go on a DIET !

MeeMee replied, "Ah, Teddy is not that fat. With his broad shoulders, he looks like a football player."

You retorted, "Teddy is just plain obese."
OBESE !!! WHAT ??? ME ?? !!!

My Grand-MeeMee used to recite,
"Sticks and stones may break your bones,
but names will never hurt you."

UNTRUE !!!
    FALLACIOUS !!!
        MY EGO was bruised.

Methinks, "It is all a matter of relativity. The cat one stands next to plays an important part in the portly question."

To prove this, I am sending you two photos of cats whose pictures were in the newspaper. One is of Percy, who weighs 27 pounds; the other is of a lost cat who weighs 44 pounds. That one was so chubby he got stuck in someone's doggy door.

# TEDDY'S THEORY OF RELATIVITY

One FOT (fat orange tabby) + One HGT (huge gray tabby) = One HXLF (humongous extra large feline)

Gee willikers, Dr. Michaelson, COMPARED to THEM, I LOOK THIN !

From my standpoint, seventeen pounds is not OBESE.

I would really appreciate it if you would call me pleasantly plump. That would be certainly true.

I AM pleasant.

I AM plump.

Indubitably, we can concur that PLUMP is less acrimonious than OBESE.

Signed:

Not so Tubby Tabby,

Teddy

# CHAPTER 4
## PETULANT

Dear Doctor Michaelson,

I am piqued.

PETulant, actually !

Yesterday MeeMee was conversing about cats with one of her co-workers, Reneé Marie.

At one point in the conversation, MeeMee told Reneé Marie that your office has me listed as a DSH, domestic shorthair. Reneé Marie was somewhat astounded.

She said, "I am surprised. DSH's have rounder faces. Many are usually grayish and white in color. Teddy is not a DSH. He is a tabby. In reality, he should be listed as F O T instead, FAT ORANGE TABBY."

FOT ?
ME ??
THE LINEBACKER ?

Doctor Michaelson, I got wind of that acronym, and I like it NOT ONE BIT.

BROAD-SHOULDERED
is NOT a synonym for
FAT.

I'm a fairly mellow fellow.
I live in a house.
My hair is short.
That sounds like Domestic Short Hair to me.

Truthfully, I am a bit rotund; nevertheless, I do not want to be listed as a FOT.

I need your advice on how to answer the following question:

How can I prove to Reneé Marie that I am undeniably a DSH ?

Best Regards,

Teddy

**Tormented Target of Witticisms**

Mirror , mirror on the wall,

who is not the tubbiest tabby of them all ?   TEDDY

# CHAPTER 5
## ALIAS

Dear Doctor Michaelson,

Pretty soon MeeMee will be making arrangements for me to come in to get my shots.

SOS

If you let me know the exact date and time, I will be sure to disappear on that day. Vanishing in plain sight is one of my unique talents.

To make a long story short, I was really writing to tell you that I am contemplating changing my name from Teddy to Red. I distinctly remember the time MeeMee brought me in with "sores" in my mouth. The conversation went like this:

Dr. Michaelson: "Why did you bring Teddy in?"
MeeMee: "He has sores in his mouth."
Dr. Michaelson: "Those aren't sores. He's a redhead. Those are freckles."

For that reason, I reckon I have the right to change my name from Teddy to Red. After all, you said I was a redhead. That way no one can call me a FOT.

On second thought, this is possibly not such a good idea either. Reneé Marie will start calling me a Fat Red Tabby.
I have lived with humans long enough to know they always take shortcuts. They won't say, "Teddy is a FRT." No siree, they will shorten it to "Teddy is a FeRT." That is almost as dreadful as FOT.

Frankly, Doctor Michaelson, I think those letters stink.

The best solution is for me to dye my fur yellow.

You can then call me

Blondy, F Y T,

Fat Yellow Tabby.

Humans will pronounce that as either

Fit or Fight.

Undoubtedly, I am quite capable of doing both.

To be blond will be an amusing experience.

It has been said,

"Blonds have more fun."

At this point in our relationship, the time has come that I should inform you about my education.

When I was a kitten, I matriculated in Mensa-Cats Academy.

Television and computers were not simply entertainment electronics for me. They were a treasure trove of information, inspiring me to learn and to discern. The history channel and other educational programs captivated me.

To become more erudite, I used MeeMee's computer to Google information.

I learned from the Masters, graduated top of my class, and was elected to be valedictorian at our commencement ceremony.

Like you, most respected DVM,
I am distinguished.
I have a degree.
I have initials.

I am Teddy Coderre, MHG

Best Regards,
Teddy, MHG
(Master of Hissing and Growling)

PS   "To your own self be true."
        No alias for me.

Now, if you will excuse me, I must get back to my arduous task of lying around.

## CHAPTER 6
### FOREWARNING

Dear Dr. Michaelson,

**Eagle-eyed MeeMee discovered my hiding place. Here I am !**

**Fortunately, I had the time and the foresight to compose this note and tape it on top of my carrier. (MeeMee did not even notice it.)**

**By the way for this visit,**

**I ! AM ! DETERMINED !      TO ! STAY ! IN ! MY ! CAT ! CARRIER !!!**

**BE PREPARED !**

**I hereby challenge you and your staff to a TEDDY TUG of WAR !!**

**(And since I am outnumbered, no scratching or biting from any of you.)**

Unyieldingly yours,

Teddy

## CHAPTER 7
### EXULTANT

Dear Dr. Michaelson,

I told you so ! I told you sooooooo !!!!!!!

Someone even snapped our picture !

**Magnificent !!**

Here is a copy for you.

You have to admit that it was

*one terrific tug of war !*

Doctor Michaelson,

I dare you,

  double dare you,

    TRIPLE dare you

to *hang our tug of war picture*

*on the wall in your examination room.*

Pleeeeeeeeeeease .

In fact, let this challenge go forth to every veterinarian from coast to coast.

Hang a copy of this picture in your office.

            Steadfastly yours,

            Exultant Teddy

## CHAPTER 8
### AEROBICS

Dear Doctor Michaelson,

Last night I had a dream. In that dream you said I was CORPULENT.

I most assuredly want you to know that I am trying my hardest to get back to my kitty figure.

It is very difficult to try to lose weight.

I tried walking back and forth, back and forth, back and forth to no avail.

Per chance, that was because I was just ambling back and forth to my food bowl.

Now I have a different method. I sing and work out at the same time.

It is much easier to exercise when someone is in a happy mood.

I am sending you a copy of my song and a picture of me, doing aerobics.

Feel free to sing the song.  It is to the tune of Freré Jacques.

"EXERCISING"

(to the tune of Freré Jacques)

Lyrics by Teddy

(Key of C)

Signed,

Teddy

The Catisthenics-Wonder

PS   I saw a picture of a doughnut-eating cat.  (No, no, the doughnut was not eating the cat.

The cat was eating his daily doughnut.)  He was so skinny.

Life is so unfair.

## CHAPTER 9
### PAWS IN PRAISE

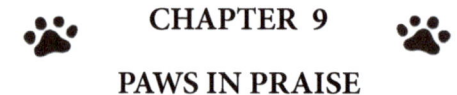

Dear Doctor Michaelson,

Truth be told, there is one day in the colorful month of November that I am jubilant to be a Fat Orange Tabby.            THANKSGIVING DAY !!!

MeeMee has a distant cousin named Shane. Whenever Shane sees me, he laughs and says, "Boy, that Teddy will make Gooooood Pickings." At times like that, I think, "Distant Cousin, keep your distance !!" (Is Mars too far?)

Good Pickings? Ponder those words for a moment. When do people actually talk about "good pickings"? THANKSGIVING ! I have a grandiose proposal. Snicker ! Snicker !! Snicker !!!

Here's your part of the plot. Feel free in November to spill "accidentally" coffee on my weight chart so my weight becomes illegible. I will be delighted to help you out.

For my part, I have been practicing and practicing a Thanksgiving ditty.
(This will divert people's attention from my size to my talent.)

**Here are the words the way my family sings the song every year before they eat Thanksgiving dinner:**

Gobble, gobble, gobble,

Plump turkeys are we.

As sure as you're living,

We'll be for Thanksgiving.

Gobble, gobble, gobble,

Plump turkeys are we.

I raise my paws in praise and thanksgiving and sing instead:

Gobble, gobble, gobble,

A plump turkey I'M NOT !

As sure as you're living,

I'm NOT for THANKSGIVING !

Gobble, gobble, gobble,

Yippee ! I'M A FOT !!!

Thankfully yours,

Non-Turkey Teddy

**PS   Sometimes Fridays can be long and dreary.  This coming Friday I am going to buoy up your spirits by joining you for lunch.  Yum !  Yum !**

**I am going to bring you a delicious cup of French vanilla coffee.  At that time, you and I can check my chart for purrmanent changes.  For this occasion, I have composed a new song.  It is to the tune of Jingle Bells and is simply purrfect.**

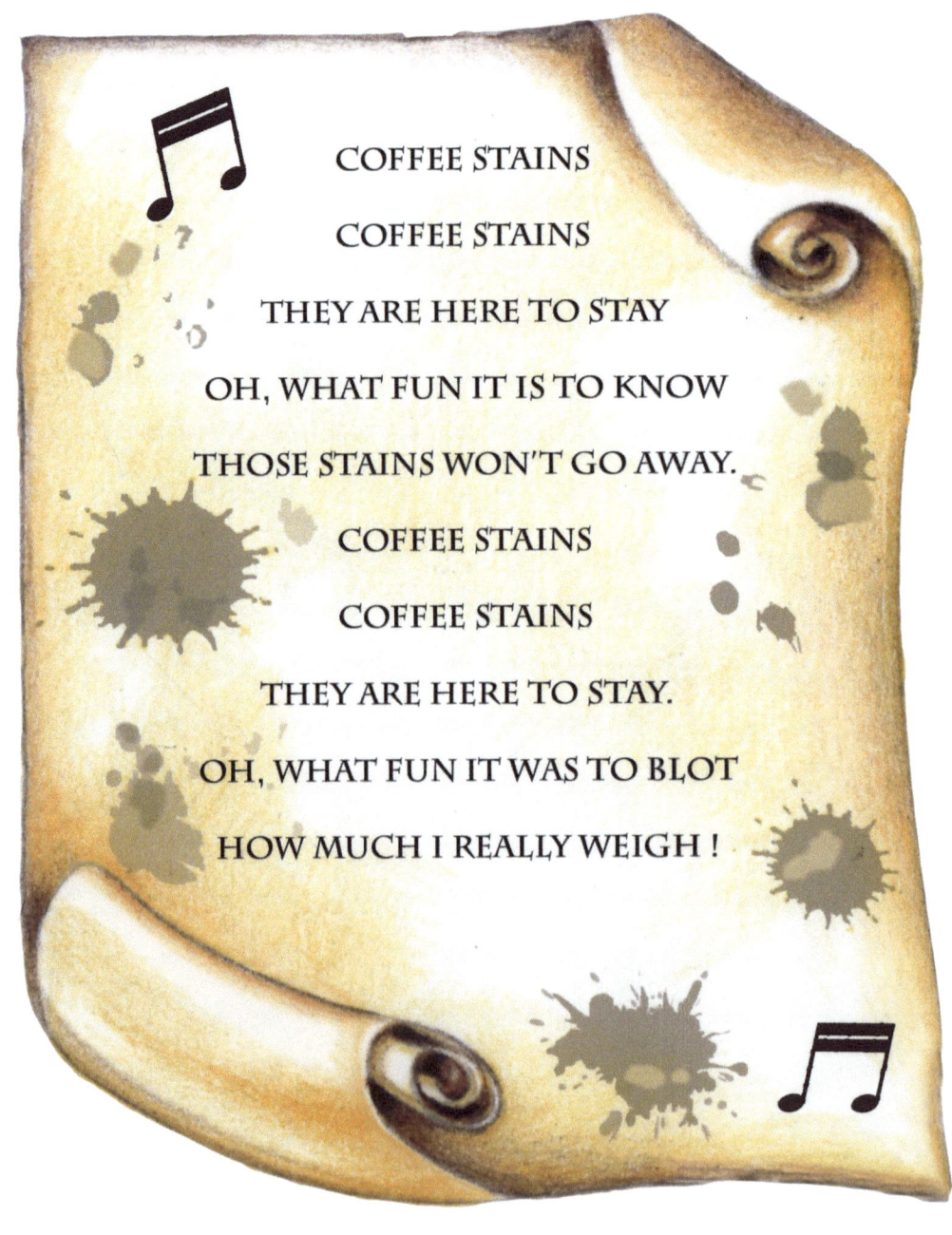

COFFEE STAINS

COFFEE STAINS

THEY ARE HERE TO STAY

OH, WHAT FUN IT IS TO KNOW

THOSE STAINS WON'T GO AWAY.

COFFEE STAINS

COFFEE STAINS

THEY ARE HERE TO STAY.

OH, WHAT FUN IT WAS TO BLOT

HOW MUCH I REALLY WEIGH !

## CHAPTER 10
### VERDICT

Dear Doctor Michaelson,

MeeMee is advising me to compose for you a letter of apology. She is also strongly suggesting that I draw a Have a Nice Day card for you and your staff.

I am doing what she requested. However, I was just going in for a removal of a little lump. But you were not satisfied just removing the lump. No, you had to check my mouth and call MeeMee to give her the diagnosis:

CAVITY

VERDICT ! Tooth Removal !

At first I was furious. Now, I have to admit that you did the right thing. I truly feel better. My mouth does not hurt. It is no longer painful to eat. (And you know how I love to eat.)

Still I want you to know that I did not enjoy that appointment.

I wrote my feelings in a song for you to sing. It is called Toothless Teddy and it is to the tune of "Old MacDonald Had a Farm".

Toothless Teddy sends these cards

Hiss, hiss, hiss, and growls.

And with these cards he sends regards,

Hiss, hiss, hiss, and growls.

With a growl, growl here

And a hiss, hiss there

Here a hiss, there a growl

Everywhere a hiss / growl

Toothless Teddy sends these cards

Hiss, hiss, hiss and growls.

Grr-URRR

Ambivalently and Grrrr-urrrringly yours,
One - Toothless Teddy

PS  To depict my ambivalence about this situation, I have invented the above new word.

Its root is a combination of grr and purr.

It is two syllables, not one.  That way it cannot be confused with an elongated grrrrrrrr.

To learn this new word, say it three times.

Grr-*URRR* !    Grr-*URRR* !    Grr-*URRR* !

## CHAPTER 11
### SANTA - CLAWSING

Dear Doctor Michaelson,

It's that time of year again. Humans are Santa "Clawsing" me !!

It was bad enough when it began in December; now the bantering is starting in October. From Halloween to practically the next year, I have to tolerate teasing. Can I help it if I am a jolly fat cat, whose belly shakes when he walks?

I have overheard people saying I am fat and red. Santa Claws they call me.

Sensitive and considerate Doctor, I want you to be my ally in this. Do you think they are being good when the jest about my SIZE?

Maybe I should not be asking you anyway. I have not forgotten that you called me obese. YOU I will excuse. After all, you are my Doctor. You are concerned about my health.

But these other individuals are a different story. I see their ludicrous grins and hear them chortling, "Ho ! Ho ! HO !"

NO WEIGH ! Oops, I mean NO WAY !!

In the spirit of the season, I have decided to respond peacefully and jovially. Jolly gift giver that I am, I am making for these people my very own purrsonal gift. No store purchased present from me. (A wink of my eye and a turn of my head will make them know they have nothing to dread.)

```
         *
        ***
       To you
     From Teddy
    Cough! Cough!
   Haaaaack! Haaaaack!
        ***
        ***
```

Now, if you will excuse me, I must get nestled all snug in my bed while visions of catnip and kibble treats dance in my head.

Best regards,

Teddy

Disinclined Santa Claws

PS   Does this outfit make me look fat?

# CHAPTER 12
## ANXIETY

Dear Doctor Michaelson,

Over and over, I ask myself why am I writing this particular letter to you. After all, I am well rounded, and I don't just mean my torso.

A problem has arisen. It is causing me anxiety. It was bad enough when humans called me Santa Claws.

Lately, I have been receiving letters inquiring if I posed for the drawing of the cat in the Shrek pictures. This is a two edged saw. On the one hand, I am flattered. On the other hand, I am vexed. Just thinking about this makes me run to my food bowl and eat away my frustration. I am obsessed by my FOT condition. It weighs heavily on my mind. Doctor Michaelson, in desperation I am writing to you so you can give me a non-confrontational answer to my question:

    How do I respond to these people who rib me about being so hefty?

I will anxiously await your reply.

                              Signed,

                              Not so Tough Tabby

                              Ticked off by Tactless Tormentors

                              *Teddy*

## CHAPTER 13
### TREASURED FRIENDS

Doctor Michaelson appreciated my letters immensely.

"Teddy," she said, "your letters are unique. Share your wit and wisdom."

       Advice Accepted !

Dear Readers,

Life is too short to take everything so seriously.

    You got to have GRATITUDE

        CAT-I-TUDE

           TEDDY-TUDE !!!

All right.

   All right !

I had my ups and downs and I don't mean my weight.

I had lots of fun.

I had Faith.

Flower loving Faith !

Faith, the giver of a wonderfully round, nicely decorated litter box !!! It was a miniature garden inside the house ! How thoughtful of her !

Strange thing though,

Faith did not seem to appreciate it when I helped her to water and fertilize the flowers she gave me.

    She called it her flower pot.

              I called it my flower potty.

                          Oh, well. That's life. AND...

Life was a banquet. It was a time to celebrate, meow, purr, and occasionally, to hiss and growl.

But most of all, it was a time to love and appreciate all the humans with whom I shared this journey.

For everyone I met, I met for a reason. You are truly my Treasured Friends.

That's TEDDY-TUDE !!

# CHAPTER 14
## TEDDY-TAIL FLASHBACKS

Dear Doctor Michaelson,

Somebody stepped on my tail.  My whole life flashed before me.

This prompted me to examine my catshence and bear responsibility for some of the most memorable moments of my precocious kittyhood.

Because you are so compassionate, I am sharing my reminiscences and sagacity with you.
(You have my permission to impart these words of wisdom to your patients.)

In my defense, I *WAS* a kitty, and life was too much of an ADVENTURE to twiddle away my time on mundane hobbies.

Humdrum?  NEVER !
Guilty?  ALWAYS !

(To those whom I offended, please accept my sincere apology.  I am now older and wiser.)

# TEDDY-TAIL FLASHBACK #1
## CLAWING the COUCH

Since I do not talk human, I was only trying to say, "Teddy lives here and is alive and well." It also helped to sharpen my claws.

### TEDDY WIT and WISDOM:

Even though humans file their nails and post their names on their house doors, they do not like us marking our territory by clawing their things.

Claw your own cat scratcher, instead.

TEDDY-TAIL FLASHBACK #2

SHREDDING FAITH'S RUG

This is a matter of opinion. Shredding? No way, Faith ! Considerate cat that I am, I was simply redecorating and renovating your house. Shag rugs are CATchier than plain boring rugs. It was my intention to submit a picture of your new decor to Better Homes and Gardens for their cover page.

TEDDY WIT and WISDOM:

Don't redecorate or renovate human belongings unless you are "hired" to do so by said humans.

Leave the rugs alone.

# TEDDY-TAIL FLASHBACK #3
## DIGGING UP FAITH'S GARDEN

Oh, how I love to play fetch. Inside the house Faith would toss a toy mouse. I would run for it and bring it back to her. She thought that was wonderful. Outside she would make the game a little more difficult. She would toss seeds into the ground and then cover them up. Nevertheless, I always found them and uncovered them for her. This did not bring the flow of praise I was expecting.

**TEDDY WIT and WISDOM:**

Gardeners do not like anyone uprooting what they have just planted.

KEEP OUT of the garden.

I'm on a roll for the next three. Happy memories are tuning me up. I can't resist the urge to sing and dance. You can sing along with me or simply read them. It's reader's choice.

TEDDY-TAIL FLASHBACK #4

SITTING ON THE EDGE OF THE PORCH

This sounds harmless, doesn't it? Our apartment is on the third floor. When MeeMee wasn't looking, I would climb through the porch railing and sit on the other side. Our building is in the shape of a mirrored L. Consequently, I was in full view of some tenants. They always tattled on me by telephoning MeeMee to say, "Do you know that your cat is on the ledge of the porch?" Out MeeMee would run to rescue me.

This was very frustrating for me. Do you like people to tattle on you? To rid myself of these blues, I would burst forth in song:     TATTLE TALES (Tune: Three Blind Mice)

Tattle tales !

Tattle tales !

See how they squeal.

See how they squeal.

They mostly tattled by telephone.

(Oh, how I needed

To be left alone.)

Have you ever heard such a moan and a groan?

THOSE TATTLE TALES !!!!!

TEDDY-WIT and WISDOM

Like it or not, I have to say those tattle tales were right to tell MeeMee that I was on the ledge of the porch. We live on the third floor. I could have been hurt if I lost my balance and tumbled

## DOWN

DOWN

DOWN.

Stay in a safe area. Do not frighten your humans.

# TEDDY-TAIL FLASHBACK #5

## HIDING FROM MY HUMANS

What would motivate me to hide from my humans?

a.   Magic word:   VET !

   (Say but the word and I would disappear.)

b.   Alarming word:   Inactivity

Humans need to exercise. Sometimes they cannot fit it into their busy schedules. In order to help them out, I used to hide so they would have to run around the house looking for me. At such times I would silently sing:

WHERE IS TEDDY ?  (Tune:  Where is Thumkin ?)

> Where is Teddy ?
> 
> Where is Teddy ?
> 
> Under the couch !
> 
> Under the couch !
> 
> See if you can find me.
> 
> See if you can find me.
> 
> Here I am.
> 
> Here I am.

Where is Teddy?

Where is Teddy?

Under the rug!

Under the rug!

See if you can find me.

See if you can find me.

Here I am.

Here I am.

TEDDY WIT and WISDOM

Be careful where you hide.  Someone could have stumbled over me.

Worse!  Someone could have stepped on me.

Me-OW-OW-OW!

## TEDDY-TAIL FLASHBACK #6
## BRUSHING MY TEETH  (This is my favorite.)

I always enjoyed brushing my teeth.  They would sparkle.  Every day I would jump up onto the sink and faithfully use Faith's toothbrush.  Up and down, back and forth, merrily chanting:

### BRUSH, BRUSH, BRUSH MY TEETH
### (TUNE: ROW, ROW, ROW, YOUR BOAT)

Brush, brush, brush my teeth

after eating food,

Purringly, Purringly, Purringly, Purringly

I'm in a happy mood.

"BECAUSE"

Faith's, Faith's, Faith's toothbrush

Makes my teeth so clean

Purringly, Purringly, Purringly, Purringly

My teeth have such a gleam.

### TEDDY WIT and WISDOM

Get your own toothbrush. Humans do not like to share their toothbrushes.

They have a phobia about germs.

In conclusion, I have decided just to

> Repent,
>
> Reflect,
>
> and
>
> Remind you:

Every so often everything seems to go wrong.  Other times everything seems to go right.  In a cat's perspective it would be described as this:  Some days you're the mouse and other days you're the cat.  That's TEDDY-TUDE.

So, Doctor Michaelson and Readers, every so often think of me and remember how wonderful and healing it is to laugh.  Happiness is contagious.  Share it.

Best regards,

*Teddy*

(aka Theodore the Wise)

I know what you're thinking. Yeah! Yeah! Occasionally, I am a wise guy. I admit my faults ... sometimes.  After all, that is, without a doubt, TEDDY-TUDE.

## EPILOGUE
## UTOPIA

You are probably thinking, "That Teddy was paranoid about his weight." Let me remind you, Treasured Friends, of this sad but true fact:

It's a lot easier to put on weight than it is to take it off. I speak from experience.

(I'm not only a Weight Observer Advocate I am a Weight Observer Client.)

However, no matter how much I packed on the pounds, this was in my favor:

I accepted myself for the good guy that I was. I brought a lot of laughter into people's lives.

Diffident? On no occasion ! Good self esteem I never lacked.

I am now in Heaven. So, if you ever need anything,

*just* "Call off my name and I'll be there."

After all, I am now

### *SUPER TEDDY*

(That is how I see myself.)

CHERUBIC !

That doting MeeMee of mine is insisting that I let you know that I am

also

Angel Teddy

(This is how she sees me.)

# IN APPRECIATION

My tail swishes in many thanks to the following people:

Faith Damon Davison for editing this book;

Marla Pinnatoro, my confidante extraordinaire;

Barbara Mariano, my personal communications expert;

The three of you were very supportive and sincerely encouraged MeeMee, whom I loved best in all the world, to write about ME, Teddy.

Karen Marshall, who compassionately and lovingly ministered to me in my illness and drew me to a T;

Doctor Jo Michaelson, DVM, who cared for me since I was a kitty and who, in the end, lovingly and tenderly laid me to rest;

My Aunts and Uncles: William and MaryLou Coderre, Beryl Austria, (Ronald Coderre and Josephine Brady, RIP). They pleasantly succumbed to being "furred" whenever they visited us;

The staff at Montville Animal Hospital: vet tech Reneé Genereux, and my tug of war opponents, Sarah Robbins, and Lori Winslow;

Christine Damon Murtha who found a loving home for me with her mother, her sister, AND my kindred spirit who later became my beloved MeeMee;

Virginia Damon (RIP) who loved me with all her heart. She also unselfishly let me go live with MeeMee when MeeMee went to live with my Grand-MeeMee;

and LAST but not LEAST a begrudging thank you to
Reneé Marie Petruzelli who was the first to describe me as an F-O-T. (Hmmph!)

THANK YOU

# From Teddy's Photo Album

Teddy and Cleokatra take a moment to "paws" and reflect.

Teddy on the road ...

... relaxing ...

... resting.

Morning Star (Bette-Jean) resting and relaxing with Teddy before storytelling.

Bette-Jean Coderre is a freelance writer and cat-tivating storyteller. As a child growing up in Rhode Island, Bette-Jean was often amewsed by her precocious cat Tiger, who loved to watch TV, especially *Rin Tin Tin*. Prior to becoming Teddy's purrsonal public relations manager, Bette-Jean taught junior high school students in Massachusetts for umpteen years. For several years, she also worked as an assistant librarian. (Shhh !)
It is Bette-Jean's hope that *Teddy's Tail* will bring much happiness and laughter into people's lives. Bette-Jean currently lives in Connecticut where she delights people with her Native American Storytelling.

Karen S. Marshall is an illustrator, graphic designer, textile designer, AND is a fan of everything FELINE. The illustrations presented in *Teddy's Tail* are colored pencil drawings, with the occasional crayon drawing (Teddy's favorite artistic medium). Karen lives with her husband Dan in Norwich, Connecticut, where she draws, paints, and has many happy purrs with her own two kitties, Cleokatra and Gizmo. When she is not *cat*ering to her furry friends, she enjoys practicing yoga, Reiki, photography and being oceanside at every opportunity.

OUR CAST OF PURRFORMERS

Vet Office pg. 11

Cat and dog window pets:
Beatrice Bally; Pebo Marshall

Bench pets:
Smokey Schoen; Gizmo Marshall; Pax McAvoy

Under the bench:
Happy Jack Leonard; Rylie Schultz; Lucky Niedbala; Nicky Quinn; Cooper Schaffhauser; Ella Santoro

Vet clingers:
Cookie Roemmele (cockatiel); Max Paquette; Sherlock "Baby" Roemmele

Door dogs:
Sammy Knight; Tucker Pawlik; Roxy Pawlik; Juneau Kennedy Howe

Amewsment Park pg. 12-15

Trapeze kitties:
Schnitzel Strickland; Stanley Springer; Dove Leonard; Dory Smythe Gasiorek

Tight rope walker ;
Mackerel Pratt

Tight Rope Unicyclist:
Saki LaFleur

Furrtune Teller:
Sophie Park

Strong Dog competition:
Otis Lapointe; Sybil Croy (bell ringer)

Ferris Wheel:
Orange car: Alice Klammer Hatcher; Lili Percy
Yellow car: Ozzie McGlynn; Shortcake Tarvin
Green car: Matthew Springer; Petey Rowley
Blue car: Ladybug Chevalier; Roux Petruzelli; Harry McGlynn
Purple car: Blue Petruzelli; Boots McPhail; Lucas Maikshilo
Red car: Shonna Shaad; Toby Shaad; Lexy Bowen

Ferris wheel center dancer:
Maggie Maikshilo

Amewsment Park sign sleeper:
Gurney Cyr

Roller coaster riders:
Red car: Lola Muccelli; Frankie Springer
Blue car: Mona Muccelli; Juliet Kollar; Julius Bowen
Green Car: Annie Niedbala; Charlie Santoro
Purple car: Cupid Rodriguez; Mickey Sayre
Orange car: Inchworm Chevalier; Minnow Pratt

The Great Mewdini:
Joey Bond Whiting

Magician's levitating assistant:
Gretchen Bally

Magic show audience:
Zoe & Aby Marshall

Hot air balloon riders:
Lucky Bunnell; Ashley Leonard; Dandy Strickland; Tigger Stanbery; Molly Santoro; Vonda Stanbery

Band Musicians:
tambourine-Emma Bond Whiting; horn-Pippin Bowen; accordion-Watson Roemmele; drums-Buster Griffin; guitar- Mia Maikshilo; dancing vocalist-Jack Luering; vocalist-Cookie Siekierski; cello- Blackburn Smythe Gasiorek

Artist Model pg. 16
Cleokatra Marshall

Singing Dogs pg. 18
Roxy Pawlik; Tucker Pawlik

Grey Tabby Weight Watcher pg. 27
Percy Springer

St. Jude Children's Research Center pg. 67
Ellie Shaye Leonard

Morris Animal Foundation pg. 67
Donald Damon

Teddy loved children and respected all other animal beings.

In loving memory of Teddy,

some of the proceeds from this book will be sent to

**ST. JUDE CHILDREN'S RESEARCH CENTER**

and to

**MORRIS ANIMAL FOUNDATION,**

"one of the world's leading nonprofit organizations

dedicated to creating a healthier tomorrow for animals".

"May the Light always shine brightly upon your path."